Design: Art of Design
Recipe Photography: Peter Barry
Jacket and Illustration Artwork: Jane Winton, courtesy
of Bernard Thornton Artists, London
Editors: Jillian Stewart and Kate Cranshaw

CHARTWELL BOOKS
A division of Book Sales, Inc.
POST OFFICE BOX 7100
114 Northfield Avenue
Edison, N.J. 08818-7100

CLB 3519
© 1995 CLB Publishing,
Godalming, Surrey, England.
Printed and bound in Singapore
ISBN 0-7858-0229-0

THE LITTLE BOOK ·OF·

Fish & Seafood

A lovely selection of fish and seafood recipes for family meals and entertaining.

CHARTWELL
BOOKS, INC.

Introduction

Fish and seafood is undergoing something of a resurgence in popularity. For some people it is the obvious alternative to meat; others will be attracted by its healthful image; most will enjoy fish simply for the delicious and varied tastes that it offers. Fish is just as high in protein as meat, and is lighter and easier to digest. It is also a good source of important vitamins and minerals. There are many excellent reasons for eating more fish, and in recognition of this, most larger stores carry good stocks of fresh fish, both familiar and exotic. Where there is no fresh fish available, there is certainly always canned fish, and this, too, can be used in a many different ways.

Versatility is one of the great attributes of fish. As well as being suitable for cooking in countless different ways, it is also a wonderful main ingredient for any occasion, whether for family lunch in the form of a soup or quiche, broiled for a light evening meal, or served in a wine or cream sauce at a special dinner party.

One of the drawbacks of buying fish and shellfish used to be the laborious and messy cleaning involved in the preparation. Not only is fish now more readily available, but it is also usually cleaned and prepared for cooking. Shellfish, too, is available in ever greater variety and conveniently prepared for the modern kitchen.

It is important to be able to tell good fresh fish and seafood from that which has been frozen and thawed repeatedly. Fresh fish should always be the first choice for the best taste and texture, but where this is not practical, fish that has been frozen need not be passed over. A really fresh fish is slimy and slithery with a bright eye with black pupil, firm flesh and clean red gills. A stale fish looks dull, has sunken eyes with gray pupils and dirty, dark gills. Shellfish should look clean and bright. Cooked shrimp and crabs should be bright red. Lobsters and crabs should be good and heavy, and the tail and claws should still be springy, indicating that they were alive before being boiled. Shellfish such as mussels and oysters should be firmly closed if bought alive. Any open shells indicate that the creature is dead and must therefore be discarded.

A freshly caught fish is wonderful eaten with little or no adornment, such as a trout cooked over a campfire, or sardines eaten on the harbor front with chunks of fresh bread and lemon quarters. However, in ordinary domestic circumstances it is fun to blend fish with new flavors and to experiment with herbs and spices. This inspiring selection of easy and attractive recipes just begs to be tried, and will surely convince you that, as well as being healthful, fish is one of the most underrated and delicious foods available.

Smoked Mackerel Pâté

SERVES 4

*Smoked fish has a wonderful flavor and is ideal for making pâté.
Other oily fish can be used in the same way.*

PREPARATION: 30 mins, plus 30 mins chilling

8 smoked mackerel fillets, skin and bones
    removed
4 tbsps margarine
Juice of ½ orange
1 tsp tomato paste
1 tsp white wine vinegar
Salt and freshly ground black pepper, optional
3½ ounces can red pimiento peppers, drained
1¼ cups clear vegetable broth
2 tsps unflavored gelatin
2 tbsps dry sherry
2 tbsps cold water

1. Put the mackerel, margarine, orange juice, tomato paste, vinegar, and seasonings into a

Step 2 Arrange the strips of pimento in a lattice pattern over the top of the pâté.

Step 4 Sprinkle the gelatine over the hot stock and allow it to stand, to dissolve completely.

liquidizer or food processor, and blend until smooth.

2. Put the pâté into a serving dish and smooth the top evenly. Cut the pimientos into thin strips, and arrange in a lattice over the top of the pâté.

3. Bring the broth to the boil in a small pan. Remove from the heat and cool 1 minute.

4. Sprinkle over the gelatin and allow to stand, stirring occasionally until it has completely dissolved. When the liquid is clear, stir in the sherry and cold water.

5. Very carefully spoon the aspic over the top of the pâté and the pimientos, taking great care not to dislodge the lattice pattern. Chill until the aspic has completely set.

Mussels in White Wine

SERVES 3-4

Mussels make a delicious appetizer to a meal and are quick to prepare.

PREPARATION: 20 mins
COOKING: 6-8 mins

60 live mussels
1 large onion, or 4 shallots, finely chopped
2 cups dry white wine
2 tsps all-purpose flour
2 tsps butter
Salt and pepper
Pinch of ground nutmeg
2 tbsps chopped parsley

1. Wash and scrub the mussels well, discarding any that are open, and will not close when lightly tapped. Place the mussels in a large saucepan, add the onion or shallots, and wine.

2. Cover and bring to the boil. Cook about 5 minutes, shaking the saucepan from time to time, until all the mussels are open. Discard any that have not opened.

3. Strain the liquor into another saucepan. Remove the top shells from the mussels and put the mussels into warmed soup plates; keep warm.

4. Work the flour into the butter and add in small pieces to the strained liquor. Bring to the boil, whisking constantly as it thickens. Season to taste with salt, pepper, and nutmeg. Add the parsley, and pour over the mussels.

Deviled Crabs

SERVES 6

Crab makes an ideal appetizer for a dinner party.

PREPARATION: 35 mins
COOKING: 15 mins

---

6 boiled Dungeness crabs
1 tbsp butter
2 tbsps flour
1 cup heavy cream
2 tsps mustard powder
1 tsp Worcestershire sauce
Salt and pepper
4 hard-cooked eggs
Dry breadcrumbs
Melted butter
Chopped parsley

---

1. Break off all the crab claws. Crack the large claws and legs and pick out the meat. Reserve the smaller legs. Break the crabmeat into pieces and discard any cartilage and shell.

2. Separate the bodies from the large shells. Discard the spongy "fingers" and the stomach, which is found just under the head. Pick out all the meat and combine it with the claw meat. Clean the upper shells thoroughly.

3. Melt the butter and add the flour, stirring well. Stir in the cream, mustard, and Worcestershire sauce. Cook over moderate heat, stirring constantly, until thickened. Add salt and pepper to taste.

4. Chop the hard-cooked eggs and add to the sauce with the crabmeat. Spoon into the clean shells, sprinkle lightly with breadcrumbs, and drizzle with melted butter.

5. Bake in an oven preheated to 350°F about 10 minutes, or until golden-brown. Sprinkle with some chopped parsley, and serve surrounded by the reserved crab legs.

Taramasalata

SERVES 4

This classic Greek appetizer is a delicious way of improving your intake of vitamins B and C.

PREPARATION: 15-25 mins, plus 30 mins chilling

3 ounces smoked fish roe
6 slices white bread, crusts removed
Juice of 1 lemon
1 small onion, finely chopped
6 tbsps olive oil
Black olives and chopped fresh parsley, for garnish

1. Cut the fish roe in half and scrape out the center into a bowl. Discard the skin.

2. Put the bread into a bowl along with ⅔ cup warm water. Allow the bread to soak about 10 minutes, then drain off the water, and squeeze the bread until it is almost dry. Add the bread to

Step 2 Allow the bread to soak for about 10 minutes, then drain off the water, squeeze the bread until it is almost dry.

Step 4
Gradually add the oil to the fish mixture, beating continuously between additions, to prevent curdling.

the bowl containing the roe, and stir in with the lemon juice.

3. Put the cod roe mixture into a blender or food processor, along with the onion. Process until the ingredients form a smooth paste.

4. Return the blended mixture to a bowl and gradually beat in the oil, a little at a time, as if making mayonnaise. Beat the mixture very thoroughly between additions, with a whisk or wooden spoon.

5. Refrigerate for at least 30 minutes to chill thoroughly, then transfer to a serving bowl, and garnish with the black olives and chopped parsley.

Sole Surprise

SERVES 4

Serve these tasty fish parcels with new potatoes and broccoli.

PREPARATION: 25 mins
COOKING: 40 mins

8 ounces puff dough
2 cups frozen spinach, defrosted
4 tbsps butter
4 small or 2 large fillets of sole, skinned

Sauce
2 tbsps butter
2 tbsps all-purpose flour
1½ cups milk
Pinch of dried dill
Salt and pepper
½ cup shredded yellow cheese

1. Roll the dough out into a rectangle 5×8 inches. Cut into four equal-size rectangles 2½×4 inches.

2. Fold the rectangles over, short sides together. Cut out the centers with a sharp knife, leaving ½ inch all round. Roll out the center pieces on a floured board until they are the same size as the "frames."

3. Brush the edges with milk and put the "frames" on the base. Brush the tops with milk and place on a greased baking tray. Bake in an oven preheated to 425°F 10-15 minutes, or until well risen and golden-brown.

4. Meanwhile, put the spinach in a pan with ¼ inch water and a little salt. Cover and cook 4-5 minutes. Drain well and beat in half the butter.

5. Skin the fish fillets and cut in two if necessary. Use the rest of the butter to coat two heatproof-platters and put the fillets on one and cover them with the other. Place the platters over a pan of boiling water and steam 20 minutes or until the fish is cooked through.

6. For the sauce, melt the butter then stir in the flour to make a roux. Gradually stir in the milk. Bring to the boil. Reduce the heat and season. Cook 1 minute, remove from the heat, and stir in the cheese.

7. Cut out the puffed inside of the pastry "boxes" and use for lids. Divide the spinach between the boxes, lay the sole on top, and add the sauce.

Singapore Fish

SERVES 6

The cuisine of Singapore was much influenced by that of China. In turn, the Chinese brought ingredients like curry powder into their own cuisine.

PREPARATION: 25 mins
COOKING: 10 mins

---

6 white fish fillets
1 egg white
1 tbsp cornstarch
2 tsps white wine
Salt and pepper
Oil for frying
1 large onion, cut into ½-inch thick wedges
1 tbsp mild curry powder
1 small can pineapple pieces, drained, juice reserved
1 small can mandarin orange segments, drained and juice reserved
1 tbsp cornstarch mixed with juice of 1 lime
2 tsps sugar (optional)
1 small can sliced water chestnuts, drained
Pinch salt and pepper

---

1. Starting at the tail end of the fillets, skin them using a sharp knife. Hold the knife at an angle and, using a sawing motion, cut along the length of each fillet, pushing the fish flesh along as you go. Cut the fish into even-sized pieces, about 2 inches.

2. Mix together the egg white, cornstarch, wine, salt, and pepper. Place the fish in the mixture, and leave to stand while heating the oil in a wok or skillet.

Step 1 Hold a filleting knife at a slight angle and slide the knife along the length of the fillet in a sawing motion.

3. When the oil is hot, fry a few pieces of fish at a time until light golden-brown and crisp. Remove the fish to kitchen paper to drain.

4. Remove all but 1 tbsp of the oil from the wok or skillet and add the onion. Stir-fry 1-2 minutes and add the curry powder. Cook for a further 1-2 minutes. Add the juice from the pineapple and mandarin oranges, and bring to the boil.

5. Combine the cornstarch and lime juice, and add a spoonful of the boiling fruit juice. Add the mixture to the wok or skillet and cook until thickened, about 2 minutes. Taste and add sugar if required. Add the fruit, water chestnuts, seasoning, and fried fish to the wok, and stir to coat. Heat through 1 minute and serve immediately.

Snapper with Fennel-and-Orange Salad

SERVES 4

This makes a lovely summer meal. Substitute other white fish if you can't get snapper.

PREPARATION: 30 mins
COOKING: 6-10 mins

Oil
4 even-sized red snapper, cleaned
2 bulbs fennel
2 oranges
Juice of 1 lemon
3 tbsps olive oil
Pinch sugar, salt, and black pepper

1. Brush the fish all over with oil, and cut three slits into both sides of each. Sprinkle with a little of the lemon juice.

2. Core the fennel then slice thinly. Slice the

Step 2 Slice the fennel in half and remove the cores.

Step 3 Segment the oranges over a bowl to catch the juice.

green tops and chop the feathery fronds to use in the dressing.

3. Using a sharp knife, cut off all the peel and white parts from the oranges. Cut the flesh into segments, slicing in between the membranes. Hold the fruit over a bowl to catch the juice.

4. Add the rest of the lemon juice to the orange juice in the bowl. Add the oil and seasonings. Mix well and add the fennel, green tops, and orange segments, stirring carefully.

5. Cook the fish under a preheated medium hot broiler 3-5 minutes per side, depending on thickness. The flesh will flake easily when it is cooked. Serve with the salad.

Seafood Torta

SERVES 6-8

A very stylish version of a fish quiche, this makes a perfect lunch with some salad.

PREPARATION: 40 mins, plus chilling time
COOKING: 40 mins

Pastry
2 cups all-purpose flour, sifted
Pinch salt
½ cup unsalted butter
4 tbsps cold milk

Filling
4 white fish fillets
⅔ cup water
⅔ cup white wine
Large pinch dried red pepper flakes
1 cup cooked bay shrimp
½ cup crabmeat
2 tbsps butter
2 tbsps flour
1 clove garlic, crushed
2 egg yolks
⅔ cup heavy cream
1 tbsp chopped fresh parsley

1. To prepare the dough, sift the flour and salt into a bowl. Rub in the butter, until the mixture resembles breadcrumbs. Pour in the milk, and mix with a fork to a dough. Form a ball and knead about 1 minute. Chill about 1 hour.

2. To prepare the filling, cook the fish in the water and wine with the pepper flakes about 10 minutes or until just firm. Remove from the liquid and flake into a bowl. Add the shrimp and crab. Reserve the cooking liquid.

3. Melt the butter in a saucepan and stir in the flour. Gradually strain on the cooking liquid, stirring constantly until smooth. Add garlic, place over high heat, and bring to the boil; cook 1 minute. Add to the fish and set aside to cool.

4. Roll out the dough and use to line a loose-bottomed quiche or pie pan. Prick lightly with a fork and chill 30 minutes. Place parchment paper inside the case and fill with rice or baking beans. Bake 15 minutes in an oven preheated to 375°F.

5. Combine the egg yolks, cream, and parsley, and stir into the filling. When the pastry is ready, remove the paper and beans, and pour in the filling.

6. Bake a further 25 minutes. Allow to cool slightly and remove from the pan.

Skate Wings with Butter Sauce

SERVES 4

Skate wings are both economical and delicious, and make an interesting change from everyday fish dishes. Other flatfish can be used.

PREPARATION: 10-15 mins
COOKING: 20 mins

---

4 skate wings
1 very small onion, sliced
2 parsley sprigs
6 black peppercorns
1¼ cups vegetable or fish broth
4 tbsps unsalted butter
1 tbsps capers
2 tbsps white wine vinegar
1 tbsp fresh chopped parsley

---

1. Place the skate wings in one layer in a large, deep skillet. Add the onion slices, parsley, and peppercorns, then pour over the broth.

Step 3
Carefully remove any skin or large bones from the cooked fish, using a small sharp, pointed knife.

Step 4 Add the vinegar to the hot butter and capers. This will cause the butter to foam.

2. Bring gently to the boil with the pan uncovered, and allow to simmer for 10-15 minutes, or until the fish is cooked and tender.

3. Carefully remove the skate wings from the pan, and arrange on a serving platter. Remove any skin or large pieces of bone, taking great care not to break up the fish. Keep warm.

4. Place the butter into a small pan, and cook over a high heat until it begins to brown. Add the capers, and immediately remove the butter from the heat. Stir in the vinegar to make the hot butter foam.

5. Pour the hot butter sauce over the skate wings and sprinkle with some chopped parsley. Serve immediately.

Stuffed Sole

SERVES 6

This German dish is elegant enough for a formal dinner party.

Preparation: 30 mins
Cooking: 20-30 mins

½ cup butter
2 tbsps flour
2 cups fish or vegetable broth
¾ cup button mushrooms, sliced
4 tbsps heavy cream
2 tbsps brandy
½ cup cooked, peeled shrimp
½ cup canned, frozen or fresh crabmeat
2 tbsps fresh breadcrumbs
Salt and pepper
6-12 sole fillets, depending upon size, skinned

---

1. Melt half the butter in a saucepan. Stir in the flour, and cook about 2 minutes over gentle heat or until pale straw-colored. Stir in the broth and bring to the boil. Add the mushrooms, and allow to cook until the sauce thickens.

2. Add the cream and re-boil the sauce.

Step 3 Spread stuffing on one side of each fillet and roll up. Secure with cocktail sticks.

Remove the sauce from the heat, and stir in the brandy, shrimp, crab, breadcrumbs, and salt and pepper.

3. Cut the fish fillets in half lengthwise and spread the filling on the side of the fish that was skinned. Roll the fish up and secure with cocktail sticks.

4. Arrange in a buttered baking dish, and dot the remaining butter over the top. Cook in an oven preheated to 350°F, 20-30 minutes, until the fish is just firm.

Baked Stuffed Mackerel

SERVES 4

In this recipe the combination of thyme and parsley in the stuffing beautifully complements the flavor of the mackerel. Herrings would also work well with the combination.

PREPARATION: 10 mins
COOKING: 25-30 mins

4 tbsps butter
1 small onion, minced
1 tbsp raw oatmeal
½ cup breadcrumbs
2 tsps freshly chopped thyme or ½ tsp dried
2 tsps freshly chopped parsley or ½ tsp dried
Salt and pepper
2-3 tbsps hot water
4 mackerel, well-cleaned and washed
1 lemon, sliced, for garnish

1. Heat the butter in a skillet, add the onion, and sauté to soften. Add the oatmeal, breadcrumbs, herbs, and seasoning. Mix well, then bind together with the hot water.

2. Fill the cavities of the fish with the stuffing and wrap each one separately in well-buttered foil.

3. Place the parcels in a roasting-pan or on a baking tray and bake in an oven preheated to 375°F 25-30 minutes or until cooked through and firm to the touch. Serve with lemon slices and thyme.

Swedish Mackerel

SERVES 4

The Swedes adore the flavor of fresh dill and mild mustard. This combination is all that is required to bring out the full flavor of fresh mackerel.

PREPARATION: 10 mins
COOKING: 10-12 mins

---

4 tbsps fresh chopped dill
6 tbsps mild mustard
2 tbsps lemon juice or white wine
4-8 fresh mackerel, cleaned
2 tbsps unsalted butter, melted
Freshly ground black pepper
Lemon wedges and whole sprigs of fresh dill,
   to garnish

---

1. Put the dill, mustard, and lemon juice or white wine into a small bowl, and mix together thoroughly.

2. Using a sharp knife, cut three shallow slits

Step 2 Using a very sharp knife, cut 3 shallow slits just through the skin on each side of the fish.

Step 3 Spread the mustard mixture over each fish, carefully pushing a little into each cut.

through the skin on both sides of each fish.

3. Spread half of the mustard mixture over one side of each fish, pushing some of the mixture into each cut.

4. Drizzle a little of the melted butter over the fish, and cook under a preheated hot broiler 5-6 minutes.

5. Using a metal spatula, carefully turn each fish over, and spread with the remaining dill and mustard mixture.

6. Sprinkle with the remaining butter and broil a further 5-6 minutes, or until the fish is thoroughly cooked.

7. Sprinkle the fish with black pepper, and serve garnished with dill sprigs and lemon wedges.

Swordfish with Garlic Sauce

SERVES 4

Swordfish steaks are delicious and are now easily available throughout the country.

PREPARATION: 25 mins plus overnight
marinating
COOKING: 10-15 mins

---

2 tbsps fresh green peppercorns
6 tbsps lemon juice
4 tbsps olive oil
Freshly ground sea or kosher salt
4 swordfish steaks
1 egg
1 clove garlic, coarsley chopped
⅔ cup oil
2 sprigs fresh oregano leaves, finely chopped
Salt and freshly ground black pepper

---

1. Crush the green peppercorns lightly, using a pestle and mortar. Mix together the lemon juice, olive oil, and salt.

2. Place the swordfish steaks in a shallow,

Step 1 Lightly crush the green peppercorns using a pestle and mortar.

Step 3
Marinate the swordfish steaks overnight, after which they should be opaque.

ovenproof dish and pour the lemon and oil mixture over each steak. Refrigerate overnight, turning occasionally until the fish becomes opaque.

3. Using a blender or food processor, mix together the egg and garlic.

4. With the machine still running, gradually pour the oil through the funnel in a thin, steady stream onto the egg and garlic mixture. Continue to blend until the sauce is thick.

5. Preheat a broiler to hot and arrange the swordfish on the broiler pan, sprinkle with the oregano and season well. Cook 10-15 minutes under a preheated hot broiler, turning them frequently, and basting with the lemon-and-pepper marinade.

6. When the steaks are cooked, place on a serving dish, and spoon the garlic mayonnaise over them to serve.

Fish Milanese

SERVES 4

These fish, cooked in the style of Milan, have a crispy crumb coating and the fresh tang of lemon juice.

PREPARATION: 10 mins plus 1 hr marinating
COOKING: 6 mins

---

4 large or 8 white fish fillets, skinned
2 tbsps dry vermouth
6 tbsps olive oil
1 bayleaf
Seasoned flour, for dredging
2 eggs, lightly beaten
Dry breadcrumbs
Oil for shallow frying
6 tbsps butter
1 clove garlic, crushed
2 tsps chopped parsley
1 tsp chopped fresh oregano
2 tbsps capers
Juice of 1 lemon
Salt and pepper
Lemon wedges and parsley, to garnish

---

1. Place the fish fillets in a large, shallow dish. Combine the vermouth, oil, and bayleaf in a small saucepan and heat gently. Allow to cool completely and pour over the fish. Leave the fish to marinate about 1 hour, turning them occasionally.

Step 3 Dip or brush the fillets with the beaten egg and press on the breadcrumb coating firmly.

2. Remove the fish from the marinade, and dredge lightly with the seasoned flour.

3. Dip the fillets into the beaten eggs to coat, then into the breadcrumbs, pressing the crumbs on firmly.

4. Heat the oil in a large skillet. Add the fillets and cook slowly for about 3 minutes on each side, until golden-brown. Remove and drain on kitchen paper.

5. Drain the oil from the skillet and wipe it clean. Add the butter and the garlic, and cook until both turn a light brown.

6. Add the herbs, capers, lemon juice, and seasoning and pour immediately over the fish. Garnish with lemon wedges and sprigs of parsley.

Salmon Quiche

SERVES 4-6

Canned salmon or tuna also make a good filling for this flan.

PREPARATION: 10 mins
COOKING: 40-45 mins

Puff dough
2 tsps cornstarch
⅔ cup milk
Salt and pepper
1 tbsps butter
2 cups flaked, cooked fresh salmon
1 egg, lightly beaten
Dill sprigs, for garnish

---

1. Roll the dough out into a square large enough to line a greased 8-inch pie plate or quiche dish. Trim off the excess dough and crimp the edges.

2. Mix the cornstarch with 1 tbsp of the milk, bring the rest to the boil, pour a little into the cornstarch mix, stir well, and add to the pan.

3. Return to the boil and cook 1 minute, stirring constantly. Season well with salt and pepper and add the butter. Remove the pan from the heat and add the egg, beating it in thoroughly.

4. Pick over the salmon, removing any bones and skin, fold it into the sauce, and spoon into the pastry case. Bake in an oven preheated to 375°F 35-40 minutes, or until the filling is firm and the pastry golden. Serve garnished with dill sprigs.

Marinated Trout with Egg Sauce

SERVES 4

In this delicious recipe from Spain, the simply-prepared sauce allows the flavor of the fish to shine through.

PREPARATION: 10 mins, plus 30 mins marinating
COOKING: 20 mins

4 even-sized trout, cleaned, but heads and tails left on
6 tbsps red wine
3 tbsps olive oil
3 tbsps water
1 clove garlic, crushed
2 sprigs fresh mint, 1 sprig fresh rosemary, 1 sprig fresh thyme, 1 small bayleaf, crumbled
6 black peppercorns
Pinch salt
3 egg yolks, lightly beaten
1 tbsp fresh chopped herbs
Lemon or lime slices, to garnish

1. Place the fish in a roasting pan and pour over the wine, oil, water, garlic, and herbs. Sprinkle over the peppercorns and the salt, and turn the fish several times to coat them thoroughly. Leave at room temperature 30 minutes.

2. Place the roasting pan with the fish on top of the stove, and bring the marinade just to the simmering point. Cover the pan and place in a preheated 350°F oven and cook about 20

Step 3 When the fish is cooked, transfer to a serving dish and peel off one side of the skin on each fish.

minutes or until firm.

3. Transfer the fish to a dish and peel the skin off from one side. Cover and keep warm.

4. Strain the cooking liquid into a bowl, set over a pan of hot water, or into the top of a double boiler, and discard the herbs and garlic. Mix about 3 tbsps of the liquid into the egg yolks, then return to the bowl or double boiler.

5. Heat slowly, whisking constantly until the sauce thickens. Do not allow the sauce to boil. Add the herbs and adjust the seasoning.

6. Coat the sauce over the skinned side of each trout, and garnish the plate with lemon or lime wedges. Serve the rest of the sauce separately.

Mediterranean Seafood Casserole

SERVES 4

Fresh shellfish cooked with red wine and tomatoes makes an impressive main course to serve for a special dinner party.

PREPARATION: 15-20 mins
COOKING: 30 mins

1 onion, minced
3 tbsps olive oil
3 cloves garlic, crushed
3 cups tomatoes, skinned, seeded, and
  chopped
2 tbsps tomato paste
2¼ cups dry red wine
Freshly ground black pepper
3 cups mussels in their shells
8 jumbo shrimp in their shells
½ cup peeled cooked shrimp
½ cup white crabmeat
8 Alaska crab claws, shelled
2 tbsps vegetable oil
1 tbsp fresh chopped parsley
8 slices stale French bread

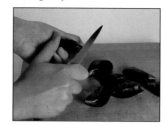

Step 4 Trim any small barnacles or pieces of seaweed away from the mussel shells using a small, sharp knife.

1. In a large saucepan, sauté the onion gently in the olive oil for 3 minutes, or until transparent but not browned.

2. Add 2 cloves of the garlic and the tomatoes. Sauté gently a further 3 minutes, stirring to break up the tomatoes.

3. Stir in the tomato paste, red wine, and black pepper. Bring the sauce to the boil; cover and simmer 15 minutes.

4. Scrub the mussels to remove any small barnacles, or bits of seaweed attached to the shells.

5. If any of the mussels are open, tap them gently with the handle of a knife. If they do not close up immediately, discard them.

6. Drop the mussels into the tomato sauce. Cover and cook 5 minutes.

7. Add the whole shrimp, peeled shrimp, crabmeat and crab claws to the mussels and tomatoes. Re-cover and simmer for 5 minutes.

8. Heat the vegetable oil in a skillet, and stir in the remaining garlic and parsley.

9. Put the bread into the hot oil and fry until well-browned.

10. Spoon the fish stew into a deep serving bowl and arrange the garlic croutons over the top. Stir briefly before serving.

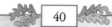

Broiled Sardines with Romescu

SERVES 4

Romescu is a Spanish sauce that evolved from a fish stew recipe. It is simple to make and has a distinctive flavor. Any small, oily fish can be cooked in this way.

PREPARATION: 20 mins
COOKING: 10 mins

Romescu (Almond and Hot Pepper Sauce)
1 tomato, skinned, seeded, and chopped
3 tbsps ground almonds
½ clove garlic, crushed
½ tsp cayenne pepper
Pinch salt
3 tbsps red wine vinegar
¾ cup extra-virgin olive oil

2 pounds whole sardines, cleaned
Salt and pepper
Bayleaves
Olive oil
Lemon juice

---

1. To prepare the sauce, combine all the ingredients, except the vinegar and olive oil in

Step 1 Mix all the ingredients together into a smooth paste, using a mortar and pestle.

Step 2 Once half the oil has been added, add the remainder in a thin, steady stream, whisking by hand.

a mortar and pestle, and work until smooth.

2. Transfer to a bowl, whisk in the red wine vinegar and add the oil gradually, a few drops at a time, mixing vigorously with a whisk or wooden spoon. Make sure each addition of oil is absorbed before adding more. Once about half the oil is added, the remainder may be added in a thin, steady stream. Adjust the seasoning and set the sauce aside.

3. Wash the fish well, sprinkle the cavities with salt and pepper, and insert a bayleaf. Brush the skin with olive oil and sprinkle with lemon juice. Cook under a preheated broiler about 2-3 minutes per side, depending on the thickness of the fish. Brush with lemon juice and olive oil while the fish is broiling. Serve with the sauce.

Index

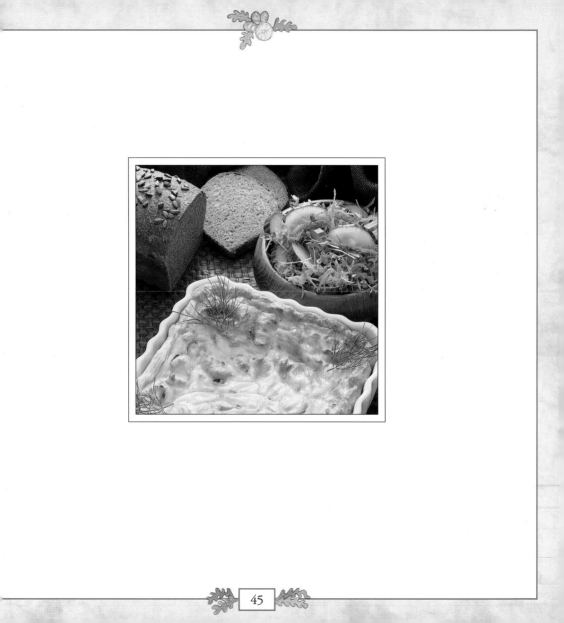